This Book Belongs To :

*To Harriet and Flying Eye, for believing
that mountains can move.*

– S.F

*To my Everest, my mom,
Weiya Zhang.*

– L.F

EVEREST

SANGMA FRANCIS

LISK FENG

FLYING EYE BOOKS

LONDON | NEW YORK

CONTENTS

INTRODUCTION

There is a place where a mountain grows. It sits cushioned between its sisters; 10 out of the 14 highest peaks in the world. Together they form a thick wall of stone. The buffeting winds of the oceans rise up against them in the spring and each year the mountains turn them away and transform the wind to rain. It is a place of invention, imagination and discovery.

This is the magic of the **Himalayan** mountain range, and the story of the mountain that is tallest of them all...

MOUNT EVEREST

BELOW THE SURFACE

Once upon a time, the planet we live on looked very different from how it does today. Around 300 million years ago, the continents locked together to form a huge mass of land called Pangea.

There were no countries, no borders, no people, no dinosaurs.

CTONIC SHIFT

over 100 million years the lands stayed locked,
under the surface the Earth's crust was slowly
ting. Liquified rock, known as molten lava, from
Earth's core was causing the **tectonic plates**
er the sea bed to drift and collide. The ground
moving, volcanic eruptions cracked the Earth,
over time Pangea splintered apart.

INDIAN
CONTINENT

EURASIAN
CONTINENT

HIMALAYAS

Around 50 million years ago, the country we now know as India gradually
collided with the Eurasian continent. The ground in between began to
rise and formed the biggest mountain range on Earth. It is still alive
and still moving, and each year it grows up to a third of an inch taller

THE HIMALAYAN MOUNTAIN RANGE

Everest rises out of two countries: Tibet and Nepal.

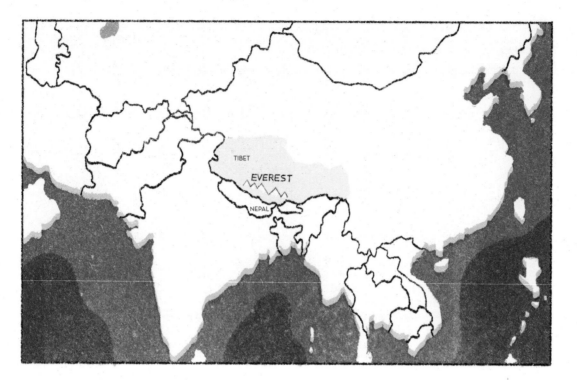

Tibetans call her Chomolungma, or 'Mother Goddess of the World'.

In Nepal she is Sagarmatha, or 'Goddess of the Sky'.

In the western world, Everest was once called Peak XV and was renamed in 1865 after Sir George Everest, a Welsh surveyor who was head of the **Great Trigonometrical Survey**.

The Himalayas stretch from Pakistan in the west to China in the east, with over 110 peaks prickling 2,500 km of sky. Even at 50 million years old, the Himalayas is the youngest mountain range on Earth. The word Himalaya comes from Sanskrit, an ancient language of India. In Sanskrit 'hima' means 'snow' and 'laya' means 'abode'. The home of snow.

हिमालय

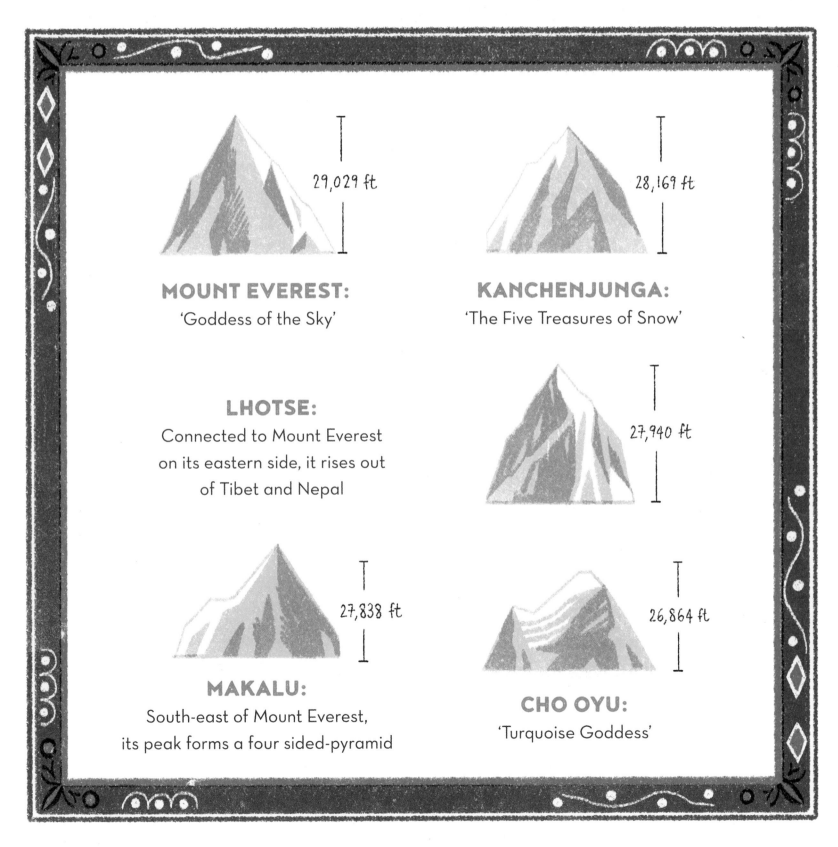

MOUNT EVEREST:
'Goddess of the Sky'
29,029 ft

KANCHENJUNGA:
'The Five Treasures of Snow'
28,169 ft

LHOTSE:
Connected to Mount Everest on its eastern side, it rises out of Tibet and Nepal
27,940 ft

MAKALU:
South-east of Mount Everest, its peak forms a four sided-pyramid
27,838 ft

CHO OYU:
'Turquoise Goddess'
26,864 ft

HOW DO YOU MEASURE A MOUNTAIN?

Mount Everest is the tallest in the world when measured from sea level. Mountains can be measured from their base, which sometimes stretches deep down into the sea, or they can be measured from sea level. But how do you measure something as big as a mountain?

TRIANGLES

In 1802 a project called the **Great Trigonometrical Survey** was set up to measure the whole of India. This was a mighty task. India is huge and covered in great jungles, rivers, hills and mountains. Some of these areas had never been explored by humans, but a simple mathematical equation using triangles meant that surveyors didn't have to. Using triangles to measure distances and heights is called **triangulation**.

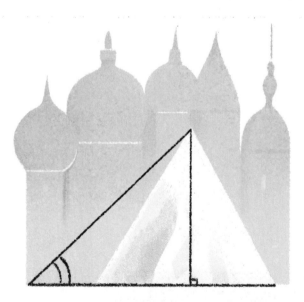

INSTRUMENTS

A baseline between two fixed points was measured across the land using a specially constructed iron chain. Hundreds of baselines were made in this way across India. From this baseline, an instrument called a **theodolite** measured the angle to another point, such as the top of a mountain.

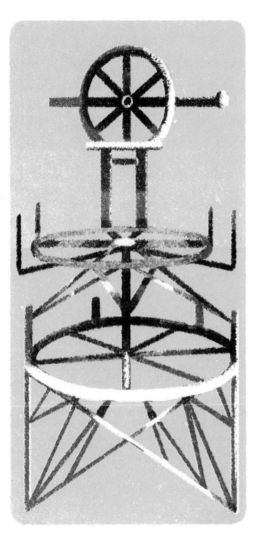

A theodolite is used to measure angles. From a baseline across the land, and a vertical line upwards, the theodolite can measure angles and calculate great distances.

A zenith sector is a type of telescope used to measure an accurate line from a zenith. This is usually a point in the sky above the observer.

RADHANATH SIKDAR

From afar Mount Everest doesn't seem like the highest peak. It was finally in 1856 that it was identified as far higher than any other mountain measured. The discovery was made by an Indian surveyor and brilliant mathematician called Radhanath Sikdar. He was part of the survey and working from a baseline more than 100 miles away when he made the discovery.

LOOKING UP TO THE MOUNTAIN

Up to 10,000 feet

FORESTED FEET

Far below Mount Everest's peak, there is a world of life. The broad-leafed forests of the Eastern Himalayas are home to an enormous mixture of plants and trees. These forests are an **ecoregion**, a natural community that shares similar plants, wildlife, temperature, rainfall and soil.

The Himalayan owl

The green-backed tit

The Arunachal macaque monkey

MONSOON SEASON

From June to September, the heavy wind from the Indian Ocean creates torrents of rain. This monsoon rain helps to shape the type of plants that grow here. Many of the birds and mammals that live here move up and down the mountain in the seasons.

MAGIC IN MEDICINE

Early explorers of these forests discovered some of the most ancient medicines of our planet. The snakeroot plant found here is filled with an important chemical called reserpine, which can be used against snake poison and insect stings. And the Himalayan mayapple has components that can be used in cancer-curing medicine.

Rhododendrons

Himalayan mayapple plant

Snakeroot plant

LIFE AT THE FOOT OF THE MOUNTAIN

The forests of the Himalayas form the **habitat** for hundreds of different species of birds, mammals, fish and insects. A habitat is the natural home for a living creature. The mountain helps create an environment that is completely unique. There are many animals and plants that are **endemic** to the region. This means they are only found in certain areas.

The clouded leopard

The golden langur

ENDEMIC ANIMALS

The wooly flying squirrel

20

HOW OLD ARE THE NEW THINGS WE DISCOVER?

Scientists are still discovering many new species of plants and animals, hidden in the deep forests of the Eastern Himalayas.

The vibrant blue dwarf 'walking' snakehead fish sucks in air from the surface of the water despite having gills.

A type of frog was discovered with menacing tusks unlike any other. In the leafy undergrowth you can barely see its camouflaged body because the folds of its skin are like the veins of a leaf.

In the trees, monkeys with upturned noses were discovered. When it rains, the water fills the noses of these snub-nosed monkeys and causes them to sneeze. They spend rainy days with their heads tucked into their knees, keeping their noses dry.

But the animals and plants of the Himalayas are now in danger. Changes to their habitats mean that many of the animals are being wiped out. The precious forests where the animals make their homes are being cut down and with it the animals are disappearing.

SACRED MOUNTAIN

Mount Everest is a sacred place for many cultures. Throughout the valleys and passes leading to its peak lie places of worship and prayer. The two main religions of the region are **Hinduism** and **Buddhism**.

Hinduism is one of the oldest religions in the world. There are hundreds of gods in Hinduism, each with their own stories. Hindus also believe in reincarnation, the idea that we are all reborn and that our actions will shape who or what we are in the next life.

Buddhists do not believe in a god, but follow the teachings of the Buddha, a holy teacher who guides followers towards peace in a world of suffering. Buddhists meditate to clear their mind of thought and reach a state of enlightenment.

TEMPLES

The village of Tengboche, in the Khumbu valley, is home to the largest Gompa in the region. This is a Buddhist monastery where climbers must pay their respect to the mountain. There are no roads to the monastery, so visitors must trek across the Dudh Kosi river and up the stony ridges to reach its holy steps.

MUKTINATH TEMPLE

In the valley near the Kali Gandaki river there is a temple visited by both Buddhists and Hindus. Both religions pray under the same roof despite their different beliefs. Tibetan Buddhists believe that the Muktinath Temple is the home of Sky Dancers (angels) called Dakinis.

THE SHERPA PEOPLE OF KHUMBU VALLEY

In the mountain passes under the icy watch of Everest, the **Sherpa** people have lived for years in the Khumbu Valley. The word 'sherpa' means 'easterner'. It refers to the Sherpa **migration**, moving from Tibet and further east in around the 12th century. They were once nomads travelling across the higher Himalayas.

Traditionally, Sherpas farm the meadows, moving their herds of animals up and down as the seasons get colder and warmer. They trade in wool, salt and seeds.

TRADITIONAL CLOTHING

Tetung

Kara

Kanam

Chhuba

MEN

Raatuk

Metil

Tongkok

WOMEN

SHERPAS TODAY

Today, Sherpas are famous for being extraordinary mountaineers. Studies have even found that their bodies are better suited to the high mountains because they are able to breathe well at high altitudes.

Sherpas have lived on the mountains for so many years that they know the land and how to survive on it.

PRAYER FLAGS

These are hung up high and each of the five colours represent the five elements: fire, water, air, earth, wind.

CHORTENS

These are dotted all over the Himalayan passes and are built to pay respect to the memory of Buddhist Llamas.

THE LEGEND OF SHAMBHALA

There are many legends surrounding the mountains, but none as mysterious and exciting as the legend of Shambhala...

Folded into the unknown corners of the Himalayas, there is rumored to be a kingdom called Shambhala. It lies between eight snow-capped peaks, with the 'near lake' to the east and the 'white lotus lakes' to the west. Each of the lakes is filled with glimmering jewels that tease travelers that have come to find the city. But greed and fortune have no place in Shambhala. Only the pure of heart can enter, and those looking to steal from the lakes will never be granted entry. Its people are healthy and peaceful under the reign of the Kalki, the kings of Shambhala. For centuries the Kalki rule fairly, each leading for 100 years.

But the day will soon come when Shambhala will be disrupted. There will be an age when men and women of the world will be overcome by darkness and greed. They will raise up their flags and march across the lands, spreading the darkness to all they come across. When this happens, when the world is at its feet, the mists around Shambhala will rise. The armies of the Kalki will come forward and fight to restore balance and goodness where once the darkness fell.

EVEREST'S ALPINE WORLD

10,000 feet and above

WHAT IS THE ALPINE ENVIRONMENT?

An **alpine** tree line is the highest height that can sustain trees; higher up it is too cold, or the snow cover lasts for too much of the year. As we creep higher up the mountain, the landscape changes. Plants need water, air, light and nutrients from the soil to grow. But alpine life has found a clever way to survive here, even in the extreme cold and wind.

MEADOWS

Meadows and grasslands stretch out within valleys where vegetation grows no higher than five feet. The soil is poor in nutrients and the land can be completely blanketed in snow for up to 6 months of the year. Plants that grow here survive by growing closer to the ground, away from cold winds.

PLANTS THAT SNUGGLE

A particular kind of juniper tree (*juniperus squamata*) grows here and at heights as high as 16,000 feet. The juniper tree mixes with rhododendrons so that each plant can act as a barrier against the cold. Moss also grows in clumps called cushions. It grows into a thick spongey carpet that keeps it warmer. Instead of roots, moss has tiny hair-like strands that soak up water above the solid layer of land that is permanently frozen.

SNOWY PLANTS

The snow lotus (*Saussurea lappa*) grows high up in the mountains where snow covers the ground. The tusks of wooly hair around the purple flower are a clever little feature which keeps it warm and lessens the damage from frostbite at night.

SMALL BUT HARDY

Most impressive of all is the **lichen** that survive so high. Lichen can live on the surface of bare rock! It lives off the air and moisture from above. Lots of lichen is red in color so that it can absorb more light for warmth.

ALPINE ANIMALS

Animals on the mountain have also adapted to the environment. These are creatures that live in Everest's shadow. They know the land that leads up to its peak and they can survive the dangers of its harsh climate.

THE SNOW LEOPARD

This is the home of the beautiful snow leopard. They are shy and rare beasts to spot. Their fur is thick to keep out the cold, and their wide feet and long tails give them balance on the soft uneven snow. They can kill animals up to three times their weight and can jump as far as 50 feet.

THE HIMALAYAN TAHR

This small goat-like mammal can live as high as about 16,000 feet. They sport a long dark upper coat and a thick undercoat. Their hooves have rubbery inner cores to help them grip the steep mountain ridges.

THE HIMALAYAN MUSK DEER

Unlike normal deer, musk deer do not have horns but a large set of overgrown tusks. The males are hunted by humans because they produce a scent called musk, which is used in perfume. Sadly, it is an **endangered** animal which means it is at risk of disappearing forever.

THE HIMALAYAN PIKA

This little creature resembles a tailless rabbit. It has extremely furry feet for warmth with five toes in front and only four toes at the back. In winter, the pika buries its food in stores called hay piles. They even eat other animals' poo for nutrients. Pikas love the cold and can't stand the warmth.

ICE GIANTS

In the most remote spaces of the Himalayas and up to Everest's peak, there are giant rivers of snow and ice called **glaciers**. Thousands of years of snow-fall has transformed into layers of compact ice, dozens of feet deep, constantly moving under its own weight.

The 15,000 or so glaciers of the Himalayas feed into Asia's great rivers including the Ganges, Indus, Mekong and Yangtze.

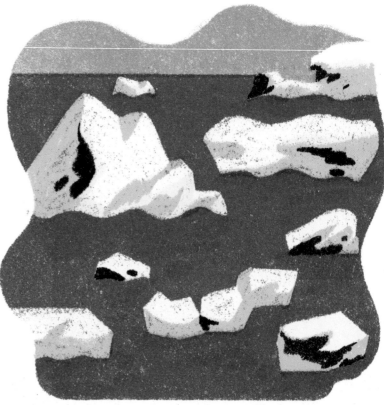

WHY DO THE GLACIERS LOOK BLUE?

Glacial ice can sometimes appear blue because the ice is so dense. It only absorbs a small amount of red light from the sun, and scatters back the blue to give the bluish tint that we see. When ice is white, it usually means that there are many tiny air bubbles trapped in the ice.

WHERE DO OUR RIVERS FLOW FROM?

If glaciers are the beating heart of the land then the rivers are its veins. They pump water around and supply the lifeblood that every human, animal and plant needs to survive. When the summer heat dries the land and there is little rain, the glacial stores feed water back into the land below.

CLIMATE CHANGE

Areas that were once covered in thick sheets of snow and ice are now disappearing as the planet is getting warmer. This is due to something called **climate change**, which is happening all over the world. As our planet gets warmer, animals like the pika will have to move to places that might not have the food they need to survive. And the glaciers which hold almost 75% of the world's fresh water supply are cracking and melting to form glacial lakes in the mountains. If these lakes overflow and the waters burst they threaten the villages, plants and wildlife below.

THE LEGEND OF GANGA

In Hindu mythology, the legend of Ganga the Goddess tells the importance of the rivers that flow here.

Ganga was a powerful Goddess that once flowed through the heavens, twisting her waters through the currents of air.

In a time of war the land of India was ruled by an arrogant king. A prince named Baghiratha prayed for Ganga to fall to earth and purify the wickedness that clouded the land. Baghiratha's prayers were heard by the mighty Lord Brahma who took pity on the young king. Brahma ordered Ganga to fall to earth, but this was not what she wanted. Ganga was furious. What an insult it was to have to descend! She could not disobey the mighty Brahma but vowed that with her fall she would destroy all that lay below. Her great waters would strike the earth and crush all that they touched.

Brahma warned Baghiratha of Ganga's fury and told him to pray to the Lord Shiva who might be able to help. When the time came for Ganga to fall Shiva acted swiftly and caught her in the tangles of his hair. The waters that came plummeting down, ebbed through his locks and came flowing out in seven streams, touching lightly down onto the ground.

The river Ganges flows from the western Himalayas for 1,560 miles through India and Bangladesh and filters out to make the biggest delta in the world in the Bay of Bengal. Over time, it has become the fifth most polluted river on the planet which affects all the people and wildlife that rely on it.

THE HUMBLE YAK

These majestic creatures are kings of the mountain passes. Quietly, they have borne the loads of thousands of climbers over hundreds of years. Without the yak, Sherpas would not have been able to travel the great distances from Tibet into the land of Everest.

WHAT MAKES THESE CREATURES SO SPECIAL?

Yaks are mammals that live at the highest altitudes in the world. Their lungs are very large so they can absorb more oxygen. Their long coats keep them warm in the coldest of winters. Under their fur they secrete a sticky sweat which tangles to create a thick protective blanket. In winter, their long horns dig through the snow in search of food under the surface.

FOUR-LEGGED MOUNTAINEERS

These silent but regal creatures can bear heavy loads up to heights of 20,000 feet with unwavering strength. Sherpas rely on yaks to live, using them to plough fields for farming. Yaks also provide meat, milk, and butter and their wool is used for clothing, ropes, sacks and blankets. Even their poo can be used for fuel.

THE LEGENDARY YAK

Legend has it that a Tibetan mountain god takes the form of a white yak. From his nostrils billow the gusts of a thousand snowstorms, and he can destroy rock, the very thing mountains are made of. With a simple wish the great white yak could bring on floods that would wash across the lands.

WHAT MAKES A CLIMBER?

Just like the yak, climbers of Everest need to be prepared for the mountain. Hiking is an important part of a climber's journey. The longest periods of time are spent hiking slowly but steadily uphill to higher ground for hours upon hours.

Rock climbing is risky business. To get up great walls of stone, dozens of feet, rock climbers use ropes, bolts and anchors to pull themselves up the mountain side in pairs. This is called **belaying**.

Ice climbers also use the belaying technique to get up sheer walls of ice. In the early days of ice climbing, they would have to use special tools to cut deep into the ice to make footholds, all while pressed up against its side with nothing but a long drop below.

BASE CAMP

Located around 17,000 feet high on either side of the mountain are two base camps. They are the first locations where climbers can set up their tents and rest before starting the real climb. To get to the more popular South Base Camp, trekkers must hike on foot, starting at the Sherpa capital of Namche Bazaar, along the Dudh Kosi river, past teahouses, tiny villages and monasteries. The ground is rocky and uneven, with little wildlife and not much vegetation.

OXYGEN

The height up a mountain is called **altitude**. The higher you go, the thinner the air becomes which means there is less **oxygen**. When humans climb great heights, their bodies start to feel a change. Even though we cannot survive without oxygen, we can train our bodies to work when there is less of it to breathe. This is called **altitude acclimatization**. The dangers of not acclimatizing properly can be terrible. Climbers become sick, their heads spin from the dizziness, and they become very weak. A climber must take time to move up the heights, so that their body slowly adapts to their new environment.

BREATHING SYSTEMS

In 1922, when the first missions to climb Everest were attempted, 'breathing systems' were made to help climbers to the top. Oxygen was held in metal cylinders in a backpack, with a tube that fed oxygen into the mouth and nose. Valves turned to change the amount of oxygen being pumped. But there were still dangers. Valves can freeze, ice can form in the tubes, and masks can warp in the wind.

THE EARLY DESIGNS

An early breathing system designed by George Finch was incredibly heavy and difficult to use. In 1922, Finch and his teammate Geoffrey Bruce reached an altitude on Everest of 27,296 feet with the aid of this system. Many years later a lighter model would be used for the first successful climb to the top.

THE HORNBEIN OXYGEN MASK

In the 1960s, a doctor and mountaineer named Tom Hornbein made a mask using the model used by navy pilots. The Hornbein mask had only one valve that provided a constant supply of oxygen to the climber and made breathing easier. Hornbein's design is still the basis for all masks used in mountaineering today.

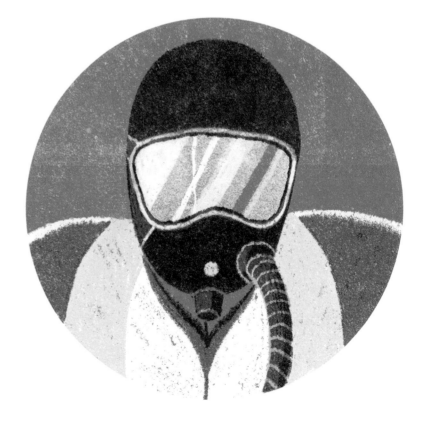

CLIMBING THE MOUNTAIN

18,000 feet and above

THE FIVE SISTERS OF LONG LIFE

The peak of Everest is a cold, bleak place where nothing can survive. The mountain stretches so high up it sits in a current of twisting air in the **troposphere** of the Earth. This is a low layer of the atmosphere where **jet stream winds** flow throughout the year. Everest's peak sits in this river of wind.

In the myths of Tibet there are stories of mountain Gods who rule over the Earth. They are the creators of the land because they hold the greatest power on Earth... the ability to twist and shape the weather, and with it everything that life on Earth relies on.

Mount Everest is the home to five goddesses called the Sisters of Long Life. Each of them rides a noble beast

and wears a brilliantly colored robe. The greatest of these is Bkra-shis-tshe-ring-ma. She rides a white tigress and her sacred arrow is used to strike the Earth and pluck the gifts laid for her on the ground. A mirror and dice made of white shell are tied to the arrow. As she rides the white tiger, her cloak billows behind her with peacock feathers that glimmer like emerald, azure and jade.

These five goddesses give fortune and wisdom to those that seek it. All climbers who make the journey to the top of Everest must pay their respects to the mountain. In the temples at the foot of the mountain all climbers stop and ask for safe passage because the journey further up is a dangerous one.

PERILS OF THE MOUNTAIN

Everest is one of the most perilous and beautiful places on Earth. It is a place of moving glaciers, **ice crevasses**, thundering snow storms, avalanches, temperatures that reach -94ºF and hurricane-like winds of over 175 mph.

WHITEOUTS

A whiteout can happen when there is heavy snowfall, a cloud, mist or fog on the mountain. In a whiteout nothing can be seen, causing a climber to feel completely disoriented.

AVALANCHES

Avalanches can begin with only a small bit of snow being dislodged, but then picking up speed and getting faster and faster. On its dangerous path down, an avalanche picks up rock, ice, trees and natural debris from the mountain.

SUNBURN

Snow and ice act as a giant reflector for the sun's glare. The risk for sunburn is greatest near Base Camp.

ICEFALL

This happens when a glacier's base becomes narrow and steep. There is nothing for the ice to do but drag, drop and crack, creating deep crevasses in the glacier. When fresh snow falls across the glacier, it can disguise the opening of the crevasse and create a dangerous trap for climbers.

SERACS

These great big ice columns can be as big as houses but still so fragile that they can topple down without warning.

FREEZING TEMPERATURES

At the summit of Everest, temperatures can reach up to -43°F and the wind chill cuts it down to -94°F. If climbers leave themselves exposed, they can suffer from frostbite. Frostbite stops the flow of blood to your extremities so that you stay warm at your core. The damage is sometimes irreversible.

THE THREE-FACED GODDESS

The very first climbers of Everest spent weeks trying different routes up the mountain. These early missions started from nearby mountains and the teams would look up at the mountain to find potential routes.

Everest has three main faces. The face of the mountain is the slope leading up to its peak. The spaces that separate the faces are called ridges.

SOUTH SUMMIT

SOUTH COL:
'col' means saddle, like a huge hump of rock.

HILLARY STEP:
A sheer wall of ice and stone just below the summit.

CAMP IV

MAP OF EVEREST
The South face going up the South Col, approaching from Nepal.

LHOTSE

NUPTSE

LHOTSE FACE:
A sheer wall of rock and ice.

● **CAMP III**

● **CAMP II**

WESTERN CWM:
*'Valley of Silence', a gently
rising valley of snow, whose
great walls cut out all sound.*

● **CAMP I**

KHUMBU ICE FALLS

● **BASE CAMP**

ATTEMPTS TO THE TOP

When the borders of the forbidden land of Tibet opened up in 1921, the mystery of what lay at the top of the world excited people from all over. **Expedition** teams from different countries prepared their best climbers and signed up the help of the strongest Sherpas to make it to the top. But the task ahead was a hard one.

1921: The first expedition to see if a route to the mountain's summit could be found was made by a British team. The climbers were the first to set foot on the mountain from the North Col. They reached a height of 23,000 feet before being forced back by strong winds.

1922: The first attempt was made, but yet again the team was forced back by the extreme weather. This mission saw the climbers become the first recorded to climb above 26,000 feet.

GEORGE MALLORY AND ANDREW IRVINE

George Mallory was a British mountaineer who took part in the first three British Expeditions to climb Mount Everest. Andrew Irvine, also British, joined Mallory in the third climbing expedition in 1924. One of the greatest climbing mysteries lies with the disappearance of Mallory and Irvine.

1924: Mallory and Irvine were sighted near the summit, but a fierce storm blew in and neither made it back to the camp that night. For years, people have searched for their bodies on the mountain, hoping to find their camera which would confirm if they had made it to the top or not.

1950: The Nepalese open up their borders to foreigners giving new access routes to the mountain.

1951: A British expedition led by Eric Shipton took a team of climbers on a mission through Nepal and up a new route on the southern face of the mountain. They had to turn back from the expedition after coming across a large crevasse they could not cross.

1952: A Swiss expedition set out, which included Raymond Lambert, Tenzing Norgay, Rene Aubert and Leon Flory. The Swiss team succeeded in being the first up the perilous Khumbu Icefall and made it 500 feet below the South Summit before having to turn back.

THE FIRST SUCCESSFUL ATTEMPT

In 1953, a British expedition was set up and led by John Hunt. Hunt was a military man who planned the expedition with absolute precision. To make it to the top, 3 tons of equipment would have to be shifted up the side of the mountain in stages. 350 porters, 20 Sherpas and 10 climbers were signed up for the expedition.

Each member of the team was picked carefully for their skill and knowledge. As well as being climbers, team members were also doctors, mechanics and scientists. While up on Everest they would not only climb, but record the land, the weather, how the human body changes and test out equipment.

1953 EQUIPMENT

While knowledge of the mountain was still filled with holes, early equipment was also quite basic and teams of climbers used gear that would seem heavy or strange for mountain climbing nowadays.

EQUIPMENT LIST

○ **OUTER LAYER:** Early climbers wore an outer layer that was thin, light and wind-proof instead of the mountain suits used today.

○ **MID LAYER:** Woollen sweaters, pullovers and shirts were used. Although they were warm, you could get very hot and sweaty in these when climbing.

○ **BASE LAYERS:** This is the important layer close to the skin, these included long johns, wool socks and wool underwear!

○ **HAT:** Climbers wore wool hats to keep their heads warm, but helmets are worn today.

○ **FACE/NECK GAITER**

○ **LOW ALTITUDE BOOTS:** lightweight, insulated with possum fur and sandwiched between leather.

○ **HIGH ALTITUDE BOOTS:** Goat leather was wrapped around the entire boot and the soles were made from a new type of rubber.

○ **LIGHTWEIGHT ALUMINIUM LADDERS:** The ladders were strung together and balanced across large crevasses to create a makeshift bridge which the climbers could slowly cross.

○ **CRAMPONS**

○ **CARABINERS**

○ **TENTS**

○ **REINDEER SKINS TO SLEEP ON**

○ **COOKING EQUIPMENT**

○ **SPECIFIC FOOD** that would provide energy and could be easily carried and prepared: biscuits, nuts, tinned fruit, chocolate, dehydrated soup, honey, ground meat and fat.

○ **OXYGEN TANKS**

○ **SCIENCE EQUIPMENT**

○ **CAMERA**

○ **BACKPACK**

○ **TRIP JOURNAL**

○ **WALKIE TALKIES**

○ **ICE PICKS**

○ **ROPE**

THE CLIMB

In John Hunt's team were the two climbers who would eventually make it to the top, Tenzing Norgay and Edmund Hillary.

Tenzing Norgay grew up in the Khumbu Valley among the Sherpa community. Norgay was a Sirdar, which is a highly experienced Sherpa guide. He was responsible for organising other guides and making important decisions about the route.

Edmund Hillary was a New Zealander and a very skilled mountaineer. He had climbed the highest peaks in New Zealand and the Alps.

On April 9th, Edmund Hillary set off to create a base camp with a team of climbers and Sherpas. It began to snow heavily but they continued onward, with many of the Sherpas using their pigtails to cover their eyes. The next day, Tom Stobart, a member of the team, came up with a genius idea. Using tape and spare lenses, he created makeshift glasses which they strapped to their heads.

On 26th April, Norgay and Hillary went up to Advanced Base Camp on the Western Cwm for the first time as a pair. All went well until they were making their descent back down and came across a narrow crevasse. Hillary leaped forward into the air and landed onto a lip of ice, but the weight of his body caused the ground to shift. Digging his axe into the ground, Norgay whipped the rope tightly around his companion, securing Hillary in place. This moment showed that Norgay and Hillary could rely on each other.

On May 28th, Hillary and Norgay set off behind the support party on their ascent of Everest.

At 27,391 feet they found the supplies left by Hunt, but they couldn't stop here. So they continued up until Norgay spotted a small flat area where they could set up camp. The support team, exhausted, descended back down the mountain leaving Norgay and Hillary far higher up.

On May 29th, at 6:30 AM, only 1,300 feet from the top of the mountain, they set off. The slope below the South Summit was the most dangerous. They decided to choose a snowy path, which was so powdery that at times Norgay sank down to his waist.

They battled on as the path continued to change and become more difficult. Finally, they got to the spot they knew was coming – a forty-foot rock face just below the summit. There were no obvious hand or foot holes, just sheer ice.

Norgay slammed his ice pick into the wall and took a firm grip of the rope attaching himself to Hillary, who then took the lead. Steadily wiggling, pushing and grabbing, Hillary took himself higher and higher. It was an incredible feat of skill and a true example of mountaineering at its best. Today this stretch is called the Hillary Step.

At 11:30 AM they reached the summit. Up at the top of the world, Norgay and Hillary only spent 15 minutes before making the dangerous descent back. But as they looked out across the vast and beautiful world below them, the two men hugged. It was a moment of celebration and friendship.

"At that great moment... [the] mountain did not seem to me a lifeless thing of snow and ice but warm and friendly and living."
– Tenzing Norgay

INVENTIONS FOR EVEREST

Over the years, Everest has inspired many new inventions. These may seem simple to you and me, but small adjustments have made a huge difference to people's safety and the way we now climb.

NYLON

Although a strong material called nylon already existed, it wasn't until the 1950s that it was properly used for climbing ropes. Earlier ropes were made of silk or twisted hemp. These older ropes were weak and could break easily. In 1953 the company EDELRID created a design using nylon for much stronger ropes. This design is still used today.

DOWN FEATHER JACKETS

In 1936, a man named Eddie Bauer came up with a design that would change outdoor mountaineering jackets. Using goose down feathers and a cotton outer layer, the jackets were warm, but could still be worn when doing heavy work. It wasn't until 1963 when an American team climbed Everest that this jacket was used on the mountain. Bauer later used the idea of feathers to create the 'sleeping robe', which is what we now use as a sleeping bag.

INTERNAL FRAME BACKPACKS

The internal frame backpack was designed by a climber called George Lowe. An external frame was awkward and unbalanced, but this new design meant that weight could be shared onto a person's hips and also had space on its sides to hold equipment, like an ice axe.

CURVED PICK ICE AXE

In 1953, the ice axe was made of forged steel and a wooden handle. It was heavy and not the easiest to use on the ice. In the 1960s, Hamish MacInnes and Yvon Chouinard separately began to experiment with different sizes and angles. The long handle was shortened, and the axe curved downwards. These newer ice picks became easier to swing over the head and could also dig deeper into the ice.

AT THE TOP OF THE MOUNTAIN

26,000 feet and above

THE SUMMIT

When Norgay and Hillary first climbed the mountain, they would have seen a yellow band of rock strapping the side of Everest's peak. Like a bracelet around the mountain's top, this rock holds a treasure: the fossils of sea creatures 400 million years old. Mount Everest is made up of different types of rock. Examining rocks can tell us the story of the land, how it was made, what once lived there and what the Earth was like.

SUMMIT

THE NORTH COL FORMATION

This part of the mountain is made up of metamorphosed sedimentary rock including phyllite. Sedimentary rock is made from layers of mud, stone, pebbles and earth that have been pushed together with great force over time. The North Col Formation sits on top of the Rongbuk formation because the rock here is lighter.

WEST FACE OF MOUNT EVEREST

THE QOMOLANGMA FORMATION

THE QOMOLANGMA FORMATION

This is the summit of the mountain, sitting above the North Col Formation at 28,000 feet. In this rock formation is a 150-foot-thick layer of marine fossils. Shells and bones that were once on the bed of warm tropical seas now sit on the highest place on Earth!

CLIMBING ROUTE

THE RONGBUK FORMATION

This part of the mountain is mainly metamorphic rock. Metamorphic rock is made when older rocks are heated and create new types of rock like marble or granite. Their name means 'change' or 'transform'. On Everest, the Rongbuk Formation is made up of schist and gneiss rocks.

HUMANS VS NATURE

Over the years, men and women have climbed the mountain and shown extraordinary feats of courage. Through strength, determination and skill they have found new routes and pushed themselves to their limits. Mount Everest urges the human spirit to soar and be at its best. But even with the many successes over the years, there have also been many deaths. The Death Zone, an icy graveyard of fallen mountaineers that lies above 26,000 feet, is a reminder of how powerful and unpredictable nature can be.

1965: Nawang Gombu, the first man to climb Everest twice.

1998: Tom Whittaker, the first amputee to summit Everest.

1975: A British expedition, led by Chris Bonington, becomes the first to ascend the South West face.

2001: Erik Weihenmayer, the only blind man to reach the summit.

1975: Junko Tabei, the first woman to reach the summit.

2010: Jordan Romero, the youngest man to summit the mountain at 13 years old.

1978: Reinhold Messner and Peter Habeler climb up the South east ridge without oxygen tanks.

2014: Poorna Malavath, the youngest woman to climb the mountain at 13 years old.

Today 18 climbing routes have been made up the mountain. There are 4 main camps to the summit, and climbers are given permits to climb in the season.

For a long time, Everest was a quest into the unknown or a challenge for mountaineers who wanted to test their skill. Today, hundreds of climbers go up every year. There are so many that lines of people have been seen leading up the mountain.

GARBAGE ON EVEREST

As more and more people have braved the mountain and made it to the top, they have each left marks of their journey. A land of white is slowly being filled with color. Shiny wrappers from food, torn material from broken tents, and glittering oxygen cylinders are slowly piling up and changing the face of the mountain.

WHAT IS WASTE?

Natural waste from humans like poo goes through a process called decomposition. When waste decomposes it rots, decays and breaks apart naturally. Man-made materials like plastic don't decompose in the same way. It can take plastic up to 450 to 1,000 years to decompose.

But even natural waste doesn't decompose properly on Everest. Decomposition needs heat and moisture. On Everest where the temperatures are far below freezing, waste stays frozen.

Snowstorms can dislodge the human waste, sending it tumbling down to lower ground. When the ice melts, the harmful waste merges into the water that drains down to the people who need it below.

HOW DO WE CLEAN WASTE SO HIGH UP?

In Nepal, climbers are being asked to bring down the waste they take up. Toilet drums have been placed at Base Camp and climbers are also given toilet bags to take with them to higher camps. Teams of people work together with a group called Eco-Everest, leading expeditions up the mountain to clean up what climbers leave behind.

THE MYTH OF THE YETI

Do you know the legend of the yeti? Have you heard of the abominable snowman?

This is the creature who strides across the mountains, appearing like a shadowy ghost in a land of white. Its shaggy, long hair covers its body, and no one knows if it is a human, bear, ape or beast.

Men and women across the ages have reportedly spotted something unknown in the mountain passes.

Some have claimed to see a shadowy figure walking barefoot in the ice — a place where no human should be without socks.

There have been visions of footprints long and wide, stretching out across the snow.

Strange pieces of scalp and hair have been discovered in rocky crags. An old, decayed finger seemed to bring the stories to life.

Some believe it is just people's imagination, but others think that the yeti will only appear to true believers. As far back as 326 BC Alexander the Great, a Greek king, searched for the legendary yeti. Many Sherpa living closest to the land of yeti are certain of a shadowy mountain beast lurking nearby.

THE SEARCH FOR THE YETI CONTINUES...

In 1925, N.A. Tombazi, a Greek photographer of the Royal Geographic Society, described seeing the yeti. "Unquestionably, the figure in outline was exactly like a human being, walking upright and stopping occasionally to pull at some dwarf rhododendron bushes. It showed up dark against the snow, and as far as I could make out, wore no clothes."

BEYOND THE PEAKS

Swooping through mountain passes, gliding up steep cliff faces, nesting out of reach: these are the birds of the Himalayas, flying over Everest's peak.

THE ALPINE CHOUGH

This is a small bird that has been recorded at heights of 31,000 feet. Their squared wings make them swift and agile, appearing like acrobats in the sky. These little birds find partners for life and lay their eggs in caves or cliff faces far from the reach of predators.

THE BAR-HEADED GOOSE

An extraordinary bird that has adapted its body for life on the mountain. Unlike most birds, the bar-headed goose doesn't soar or use upward currents of air to get higher but relies on the muscle power of its wings alone. Its heart is larger to help pump more oxygen around its body and it is able to hyperventilate, which means it can breathe in and out exceedingly fast without getting dizzy.

DEMOISELLE CRANES

From August to September, demoiselle cranes gather in flocks and prepare for their yearly migration to India. These birds endure one of the toughest migration routes in the world by flying through the Himalayan passes. In North India these birds are known as Koonj and their flying formation inspired ancient formations for soldiers in war.

IF EVEREST COULD TELL A STORY, WHICH ONE WOULD IT TELL?

Perhaps it would retell the stories of the gods that play above its peak or applaud the brave men and women who have come to meet it at the top. Or would the story be a sadder one? It might whisper about the forests that are being stripped from its feet or cry over the glaciers that no longer cover its back...

Strong as it may stand, Everest belongs to a delicate network of life on our planet, and we too are a part of this. The changes we make to the world of Everest shapes the story that it will tell.

GLOSSARY

Alpine Relating to high mountains.

Altitude The height of something.

Altitude Acclimatization The process of adapting to low levels of oxygen at a high altitude.

Belaying A technique used by climbers to pull themselves up a mountain in pairs.

Buddhism A religion that follows the teachings of Buddha, a holy teacher who guides followers towards enlightenment.

Climate Change Changes in average weather, temperature and climate which have been influenced by human activity.

Ecoregion A space that has no fixed area but shares the same temperature, rainfall and type of land.

Endangered A living thing that is at risk of disappearing forever.

Endemic A plant or animal found only in a particular region.

Expedition A journey undertaken by a group of people with a particular purpose.

Fossils The remains or traces of plants and animals that lived long ago.

Glaciers Giant rivers of snow and ice.

Great Trigonometrical Survey A project begun in 1802 to scientifically measure the whole of India.

Habitat A natural home for a living creature.

Himalayas A mountain range in Asia, containing the world's highest mountain.

Hinduism An Indian religion. It has many gods and teaches that people have another life on earth after they die.

Ice crevasses Deep cracks found in an ice sheet or glacier.

Jet stream winds Fast-flowing and narrow winds that move around the Earth.

Lava Rock that comes from volcanoes in its molten form.

Lichen It is made up of fungus and algae that work well living together.

Migration The movement of living things from one region to another.

Monsoon A heavy wind from the Indian Ocean that brings heavy rainfall to South and Southeast Asia.

Oxygen A chemical element found in the air that is necessary for life.

Sherpa A group of people who are historically native to the Himalayas. Many are known for their skills as mountaineers.

Summit The highest point of a mountain.

Tectonic plates Pieces of the two sub-layers of the Earth's crust that move, fracture and float.

Theodolite An instrument used to measure angles.

Triangulation The use of triangles to measure distances and heights.

Troposphere The lowest region of the Earth's atmosphere.

FURTHER READING

Himalaya (Vanishing Cultures),
Jan Reynolds

*Conquering Everest: The Lives of Edmund Hillary
and Tenzing Norgay: A Graphic Novel,*
Lewis Helfand (Author), Amit Tayal (Illustrator)

Indian Tales,
Shenaaz Nanji (author) and Christopher Corr (illustrator)

*It's Your World: Get Informed,
Get Inspired & Get Going!,*
Chelsea Clinton

Super Earth Encyclopaedia,
John Woodward

Almost Gone, the World's Rarest Animals,
Steve Jenkin

Order from www.flyingeyebooks.com